ENGLISH / HAITIAN CREOLE

PictureThis!
Word-to-Word
Dictionary

VISTA
SCHOOL RESOURCES

B
C
D
E
F
G
H
I
J
K
L
M
N
O
P
Q
R
S
T
U
V
W
X
Y
Z

PictureThis!
Word-to-Word Dictionary

Introducing **PictureThis! Word-to-Word Dictionary** — a captivating and educational journey into the "world of words", specifically crafted for elementary students, families, and adults alike. Immerse yourself in the power of language through this unique word-to-word picture dictionary where every page comes to life with photographs that make learning an engaging and memorable experience.

This family-friendly resource encourages collaborative learning. Parents and guardians can join the adventure, sparking conversations and expanding everyone's knowledge together. Whether you're exploring the dictionary as a family or delving into it independently, the real-life images add depth and context to the learning experience.

For adults seeking to strengthen their vocabulary or English language learners aiming to build a solid foundation, **PictureThis!** is a valuable companion. The carefully curated selection of words covers a wide range of topics, making it a versatile tool for personal growth and development.

Open the pages of **PictureThis!** and embark on a linguistic journey where words come to life through captivating visuals. Ignite a love for language, foster curiosity and empower learners of all ages with this extraordinary word-to-word picture dictionary.

Nou gen anpil plezi entwodui Diksyonè Anglè Kreyòl ak desen sa a. Liv la tankou yon vwayaj nan "lekti mo ak desen", ki pote kè kontan pou lektè yo, timoun kou granmoun. Nou kreye diksyonè a avèk anpil atansyon pou elèv nan nivo elemantè, pou fanmi yo ak pou pwofesè yo. Chak paj nan diksyonè a vini ak bèl foto pou souvni aprantisaj la rete nan lespri nou pandan lontan.

Se yon resous pou ankouraje kolaborasyon nan devlopman vokabilè. Paran yo osinon pwofesè yo kapab kòmanse konvèsasyon sou diferan tèm ak sijè ki gen nan liv la. Lektè yo ka esplore liv la pou kont yo, an gwoup osinon ak pwofesè yo. Foto yo bèl. Sijè yo ak tèm yo divès, kon sa lektè yo kapab grandi ak liv la ofiramezi yo ap aprann diferan sijè.

Annavan, ouvri liv la epi anbake ansanm nan yon avanti kote mo yo ap viv ak foto yo pou fè nou renmen lang nou ansanm ak lang Anglè nou vle aprann nan.

abandon • abandone

above • anwo

absent • absan

absorb • absòbe

accelerate • akselere

accept • aksepte

access • aksè

accompany akonpaye

ache • doulè

achieve • reyisi

acquire • achte

act • jwe wòl

A
B
C
D
E
F
G
H
I
J
K
L
M
N
O
P
Q
R
S
T
U
V
W
X
Y
Z

A

B
C
D
E
F
G
H
I
J
K
L
M
N
O
P
Q
R
S
T
U
V
W
X
Y
Z

actor • aktè

adaptation adaptasyon

add • ajoute

adjust • ajiste

admire • admire

admit • admèt

adopt • adopte

adult • granmoun

advance • avanse

advise • konseye

afraid • pè

agree • dakò

A
B C D E F G H I J K L M N O P Q R S T U V W X Y Z

aid • ede

aim • vize

air conditioner
èkondisyone

airplane • avyon

airport • ayewopò

album • albòm

align • aliyen

alligator • kayiman

allow • pèmèt

almond • zanmann

alphabet • alfabè

alter • ajiste

A

B
C
D
E
F
G
H
I
J
K
L
M
N
O
P
Q
R
S
T
U
V
W
X
Y
Z

amaze • etone

ambulance • anbilans

amphibian • anfibi

amuse • amize

analyze • analize

anchor • lank

angel • zanj

anger • fache

animal • animal

ankle • cheviy
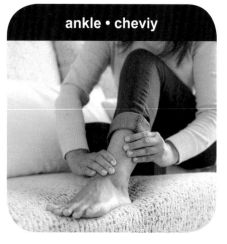

announce • anonse

annoy • annuiye

answer • reponn

ant • foumi

antelope • antílòp

antenna • antèn

apartment • apatman

ape • senj

apologize • fè eskiz

appear • parèt

applaud • aplodi

apple • pòm

apply • aplike

appoint • nonmen

A
B
C
D
E
F
G
H
I
J
K
L
M
N
O
P
Q
R
S
T
U
V
W
X
Y
Z

A

B C D E F G H I J K L M N O P Q R S T U V W X Y Z

approach • apwoche

approve • apwouve

apricot • abriko

apron • tabliye

aquarium • akwaryòm

archery • tire flèch

architect • achitèk

argue • diskite

arise • leve

arm • bra

armor • pwoteksyon

arrange • òganize

arrive • rive

arrow • flèch

artist • atis

ask • mande

asparagus • aspèj

assemble • montaj

assist • ede

astronaut • astwonòt

astrononomer astwonòm

athlete • atlèt

atlas • atlas

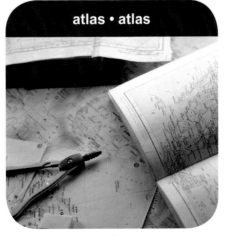

atmosphere • atmosfè

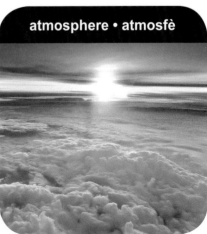

A
B
C
D
E
F
G
H
I
J
K
L
M
N
O
P
Q
R
S
T
U
V
W
X
Y
Z

A
B
C
D
E
F
G
H
I
J
K
L
M
N
O
P
Q
R
S
T
U
V
W
X
Y
Z

atom • atòm
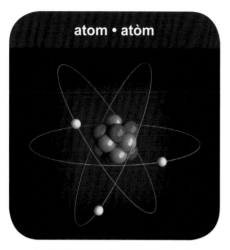

attach • atache

attack • atake

attain • rive

attempt • eseye

attention • atansyon

attract • atire

aunt • matant

author • otè

automobile • otomobil
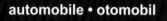

autumn • otòn

avalanche • avalanch

avoid • evite

await • tann

awaken • reveye

award • pri

axe • rach

axis • aks

baby • bebe

back • do

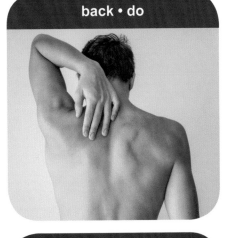

bacon • bekonn

badge • plak

bag • sache

bake • kwit nan fou

A
B
C
D
E
F
G
H
I
J
K
L
M
N
O
P
Q
R
S
T
U
V
W
X
Y
Z

baker • boulanje

balance • balanse

balcony • balkon

bald • chòv

ball • boul

ballerina • balerina

balloon • blad

bamboo • banbou

ban • entèdi

banana • fig

band • òkès

bandage • pansman
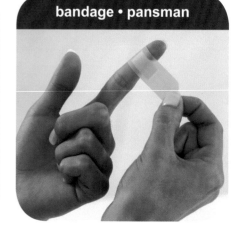

bang • ekla

bank • bank

bar graph
grafik an baton

barbecue • griyad

barbecue • fè griyad

bargain • negosye

bark • jape

barn • etab

barrel • barik

baseball • bezbòl

basket • panye

basketball
balon baskèt

A
B
C
D
E
F
G
H
I
J
K
L
M
N
O
P
Q
R
S
T
U
V
W
X
Y
Z

A

B

C
D
E
F
G
H
I
J
K
L
M
N
O
P
Q
R
S
T
U
V
W
X
Y
Z

bat • chòvsouri

bath • basen

bathe • benyen

battery • batrí

battle • batay

bay • labè

beach • plaj

beak • bèk

beans • pwa

bear • lous

bear • sipòte

beard • bab

beat • bat

become • transfòme

bed • kabann

bee • abèy

beetle • pyelou

beg • sipliye

begin • kòmanse

behave • konpòte

behind • dèyè

believe • kwè

bell • klòch

belong • fè pati

A
B
C
D
E
F
G
H
I
J
K
L
M
N
O
P
Q
R
S
T
U
V
W
X
Y
Z

A
B
C
D
E
F
G
H
I
J
K
L
M
N
O
P
Q
R
S
T
U
V
W
X
Y
Z

below • anba

belt • sentiwon

bend • koube

berry
fwi ki gen grenn

beside • bò kote

best • meyè

bet • parye

between • ant

beware
pote atansyon

bicycle • bisiklèt

big / bigger / biggest
gran / pi gran / pi gran pase tout

bill • fakti

billiards • biya

bin • bwat fatra

bird • zwazo

birthday • anivèsè

biscuit • bisuit

bite • mòde

black • nwa

blackboard • tablo

blame • blame

blanket • kouvreli

bleed • blese

blend • melanje

A B C D E F G H I J K L M N O P Q R S T U V W X Y Z

A
B
C
D
E
F
G
H
I
J
K
L
M
N
O
P
Q
R
S
T
U
V
W
X
Y
Z

bless • beni

blink • zye dou

blizzard • tanpèt nèj

block • bloke

blood • san

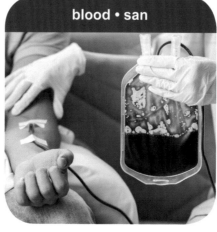

bloom • fleri

blow • soufle

blue • ble

blush • wouji

board • monte

boast • fè chèlbè

boat • bato

body • kò

boil • bouyi

bone • zo

book • liv

boots • bòts

borrow • prete

bother • deranje

bottle • boutèy

bottom • nan fon

bounce • rebondi

bow • ne

bow • koube

A B C D E F G H I J K L M N O P Q R S T U V W X Y Z

A
B
C
D
E
F
G
H
I
J
K
L
M
N
O
P
Q
R
S
T
U
V
W
X
Y
Z

bowl • bòl

bowl • lanse
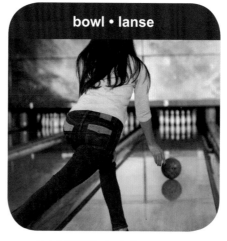

box • bwat

box • bokse
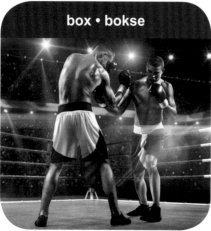

boy • ti gason

bracelet • braslè

brain • sèvo
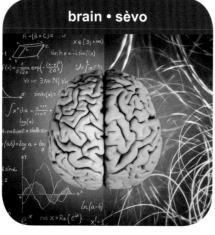

branch • branch

bread • pen

break • kase

break down • kriye

breakfast
manje maten

breath • souf

brick • brik

bride • lamarye

bridge • pon

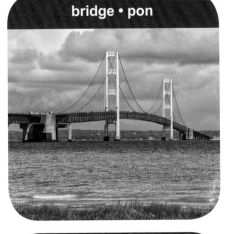

bring • pote

broken • kase

broom • bale

brother • frè

brown • mawon

browse • chèche

brush • bwòs

brush • bwose

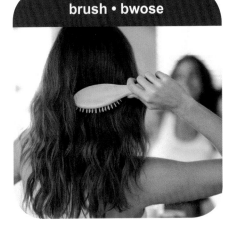

A
B
C
D
E
F
G
H
I
J
K
L
M
N
O
P
Q
R
S
T
U
V
W
X
Y
Z

A
B
C
D
E
F
G
H
I
J
K
L
M
N
O
P
Q
R
S
T
U
V
W
X
Y
Z

bubble • boul

bucket • bokit

buckle • boukle

budge • sede

buffalo • bizon

build • konstwi

building • bilding

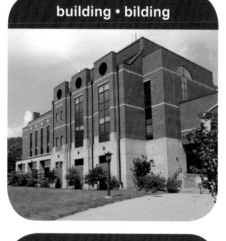

bulb • anpoul

bull • towo

bully • entimide

bump • frape

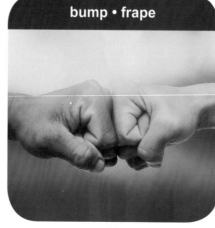

bun • pen

bunch • grap

bundle • pake

bungalow • bongalo

burger • anbègè

burn • brile

burst • eklate

bury • antere

bus • otobis

bush • touf plant

butcher • bouche

butter • bè

butterfly • papiyon

A
B
C
D
E
F
G
H
I
J
K
L
M
N
O
P
Q
R
S
T
U
V
W
X
Y
Z

A
B
C
D
E
F
G
H
I
J
K
L
M
N
O
P
Q
R
S
T
U
V
W
X
Y
Z

buttons • bouton

buy • achte

cabbage • chou

cabinet • bifèt

cable • kab

cactus • kaktis

café • kafeterya

cage • kalòj

cake • gato

calculate • kalkile

calculator • kalkilatè
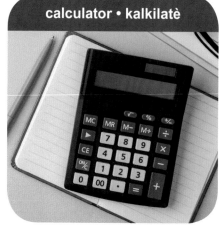

calendar • kalandriye

calf • vo

call • apèl

camel • chamo

camera • kamera

camouflage kamouflaj

camp • al nan kan

canal • kanal

candle • bouji

candy • sirèt

canoe • kannòt

cans • mamit

canteen • kantin

A B **C** D E F G H I J K L M N O P Q R S T U V W X Y Z

A
B
C
D
E
F
G
H
I
J
K
L
M
N
O
P
Q
R
S
T
U
V
W
X
Y
Z

cap • kapichon

capacity • kapasite

captain • kapitèn

car • oto

card • kat

care • pran swen

carnival • kanaval

carnivore • kanivò

carpenter • chapantye

carpet • tapi

carrot • kawòt

carry • pote

cart • charyo

cartoon • desen anime

carve • dekoupe

cascade • kaskad

castle • chato

cat • chat

catch • atrap

caterpillar • cheni

cauliflower • chouflè

cave • gwòt

ceiling • plafon

celebrate • selebre

A B **c** D E F G H I J K L M N O P Q R S T U V W X Y Z

A
B
c
D
E
F
G
H
I
J
K
L
M
N
O
P
Q
R
S
T
U
V
W
X
Y
Z

cell • selil
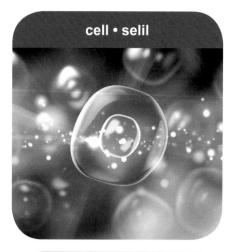

center • sant

centimeters • santimèt

centipede • milpye

cereal • sereyal

certain • sèten

chain • chenn

chair • chèz

chalk • lakrè

chance • chans

change • chanje

chase • pousuiv

chat • koze

check • verifye
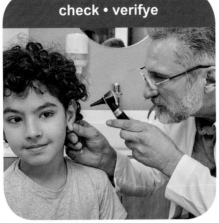

cheek • pomèt
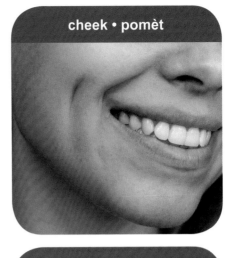

cheer • aplodi

cheese • fwomaj

chef • chèf kuizinye

chemical change chanjman chimik
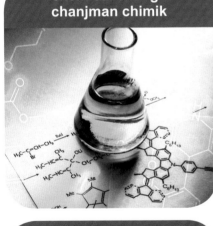

cherry • seriz

chess • echèk

chest • kòf

chew • moulen

chick • tipoul

A B **C** D E F G H I J K L M N O P Q R S T U V W X Y Z

A
B
C
D
E
F
G
H
I
J
K
L
M
N
O
P
Q
R
S
T
U
V
W
X
Y
Z

chicken • poul

children • timoun

chili • chili

chimney • chemine

chin • manton

chip • taye

chirp • gazouye

chocolate • chokola

choose • chwazi

chop • koupe

Christmas • Nwèl

chuckle • ri

church • legliz

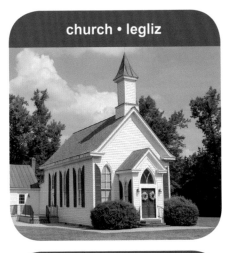

cinema • sinema

circle • sèk

circumference sikonferans

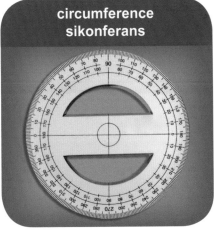

circus • sik

city • lavil

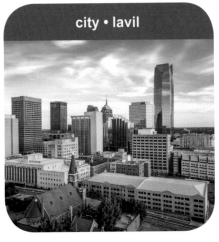

clap • aplodi

class • klas

classroom • sal klas

clean • netwaye

clear • debleye

climb • grenpe

A
B
c
C
D
E
F
G
H
I
J
K
L
M
N
O
P
Q
R
S
T
U
V
W
X
Y
Z

A
B
c
D
E
F
G
H
I
J
K
L
M
N
O
P
Q
R
S
T
U
V
W
X
Y
Z

cling • kolan

clinic • klinik

clip • pens

clock • revèy

close • fèmen

cloth • twal

clothes • rad

clouds • nyaj

clowns • kloun

coach • antrenè

coal • chabon

coast • lakòt

coat • manto

cobra • kobra

coconut • kokoye

coffee • kafe

coins • monnen

collapse • demoli

collect • ranmase

collide • frape

color • koulè

color • kolorye

comb • peny

comb • penyen

A B **C** D E F G H I J K L M N O P Q R S T U V W X Y Z

A B **C** D E F G H I J K L M N O P Q R S T U V W X Y Z

come • vini

comet • komèt

commence • kòmanse

community kominote

compass • konpa

complain • konplenn

complete • konplete

compound • konpoze

computer • òdinatè

condensation kondansasyon
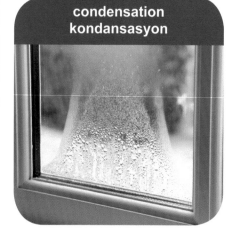

conduct • dirije

conduction kondiksyon

cone • kòn

congruent
kongriyan

connect • konekte

conservation
konsèvasyon

constellations
konstelasyon

consult • konsilte

consumer
konsomatè

container • veso

cook • kuizinyè

cook • kwit manje
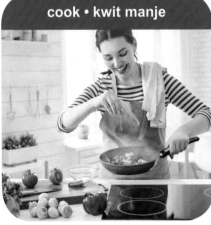

cookie • bonbon

cool • refwadi

A B **c** D E F G H I J K L M N O P Q R S T U V W X Y Z

A
B
c
D
E
F
G
H
I
J
K
L
M
N
O
P
Q
R
S
T
U
V
W
X
Y
Z

copy • fotokopi

cord • kòd

core • nwayo

corn • mayi

corner • kwen

cottage • kabin

cotton • koton

cough • touse

count • konte

country • peyi

couple • koup

court • tribinal
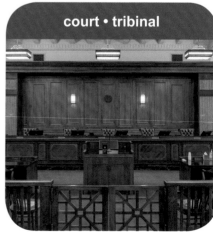

cover • kouvri

cow • vach

crab • krab

crack • fann

**crane
gri konstriksyon**

crash • kolizyon

crawl • rale

create • kreye

croak • chante

crocodile • kwokodil

cross • kwa

cross • travèse

A
B
c
D
E
F
G
H
I
J
K
L
M
N
O
P
Q
R
S
T
U
V
W
X
Y
Z

A
B
c
D
E
F
G
H
I
J
K
L
M
N
O
P
Q
R
S
T
U
V
W
X
Y
Z

crouch • akoupi

crow • kaw

crowd • foul

crowd • foul

crown • kouwòn

crumble • deteryore

crust • kwout

cry • kriye

cube • kib

cucumber • konnonm

cuddle • karese

cup • tas

curb • twotwa

curl • boukle

curtain • rido

cushion • kousen

cut • koupe

cut down • koupe

cylinder • silenn

dad • papa

dam • baraj

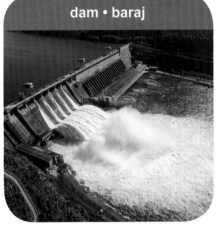

damage • dega

dance • danse

dancer • dansè

A
B
C
D
E
F
G
H
I
J
K
L
M
N
O
P
Q
R
S
T
U
V
W
X
Y
Z

A
B
C
D
E
F
G
H
I
J
K
L
M
N
O
P
Q
R
S
T
U
V
W
X
Y
Z

dark • sonb

dart • flèch

dash • an vitès

data • enfòmasyon

dates • dat

daughter • pitit fi

day • jou

decide • deside

decimal • desimal

deck • pake kat

decompose • pouri

decorate • dekore

decrease • diminye

deep • pwofon

deer • sèf

defend • defann

deliver • delivre

den • refij

denominator denominatè
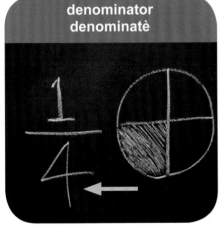

density • dansite

dentist • dantis

deposition sedimantasyon
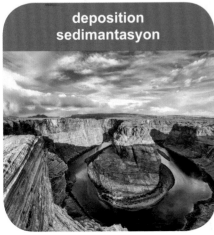

desert • dezè

design • desen

A B C **D** E F G H I J K L M N O P Q R S T U V W X Y Z

A
B
C
D
E
F
G
H
I
J
K
L
M
N
O
P
Q
R
S
T
U
V
W
X
Y
Z

design • konsevwa

desk • biwo

dessert • desè

destroy • detwi

detective • detektif

diagram • dyagram

diameter • dyamèt

diamond • dyaman

diaper • kouchèt

diary • kaye jounal
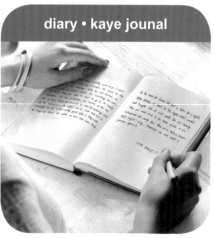

dice • zo

dice • koupe an kib

dictionary • diksyonè
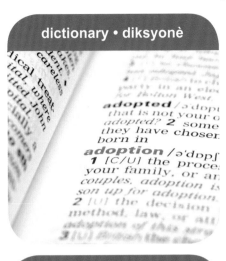

difference • diferans

dig • fouye

dinner • repa

dinosaur • dinozò

dip • pant

direction • direksyon

dirty • sal

discard • dechè

discover • dekouvri

dish • plat

distance • distans
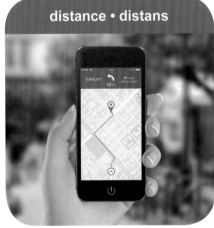

A B C **D** E F G H I J K L M N O P Q R S T U V W X Y Z

A B C **D** E F G H I J K L M N O P Q R S T U V W X Y Z

dive • plonje

diver • plonjè

divide • divize

division • divizyon

divisor • divizè

dock • waf

doctor • doktè

dog • chyen

doll • pope

dollar • dola

dolphin • dofen

dome • donm
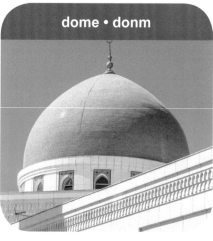

PictureThis! Word-to-Word Dictionary

domino • domino

donkey • bourik

donut • beyè

door • pòt

dough • pat

down • desann

drag • rale

drain • vide

draw • desinen

drawer • tiwa

drawing • desen

dream • rèv

A B C **D** E F G H I J K L M N O P Q R S T U V W X Y Z

A
B
C
D
E
F
G
H
I
J
K
L
M
N
O
P
Q
R
S
T
U
V
W
X
Y
Z

dream • reve

dress • rad

dress • abiye

drift • deriv

drill • pèse

drink • bwason

drink • bwè

drive • kondui

driver • chofè

drop • gout

drop • desann

drop • tonbe

drought • sechrès

drum • tanbou

dry • seche

duck • kanna

eagle • èg

ear • zòrèy

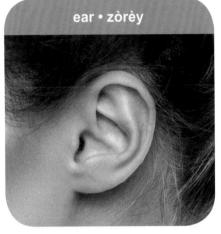

earring • zanno

Earth • Latè

earthquake tranblemanntè

earthworm • vètè

eat • manje

eclipse • eklips

A
B
C
D
E
F
G
H
I
J
K
L
M
N
O
P
Q
R
S
T
U
V
W
X
Y
Z

A
B
C
D
E
F
G
H
I
J
K
L
M
N
O
P
Q
R
S
T
U
V
W
X
Y
Z

ecosystem
ekosistèm

edge • bòdi

eel • zangi

egg • ze

eight • uit

elapsed time
tan pase

elbow • koud
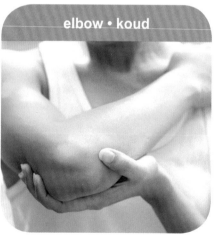

electricity • elektrisite

element • eleman

elephant • elefan

elevator • asansè

email • imel

embryo • anbriyon

empty • vid

enclose • fèmen

energy • enèji

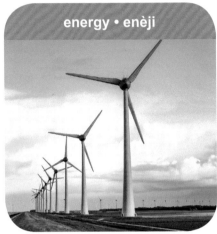

**energy pyramid
piramid enèji**

engine • motè

enter • antre

entrance • antre

envelope • anvlòp

**environment
anviwonnman**

**equilateral triangle
triyang ekilateral**

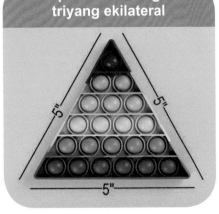

equation • ekwasyon

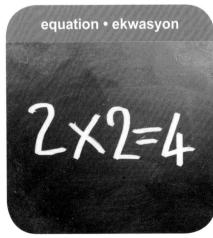

A B C D E F G H I J K L M N O P Q R S T U V W X Y Z

A B C D E F G H I J K L M N O P Q R S T U V W X Y Z

equator • ekwatè

equipment • ekipman

erase • efase

erosion • ewozyon

escalator eskalye woulan

escape • chape

eskimo • eskimo

evacuate • retire

evaporation evaporasyon

evening • aswè

examine • ekzamine

exercise • egzèsis

exhibition
espozisyon

experiment
esperyans

explain • esplike

explore • esplore

eye • zye

eyebrow • sousi

fabric • twal

face • figi

factory • izin

fall • tonbe

family • fanmi

fan • vantilatè

A B C D E F G H I J K L M N O P Q R S T U V W X Y Z

A
B
C
D
E
F
G
H
I
J
K
L
M
N
O
P
Q
R
S
T
U
V
W
X
Y
Z

farm • fèm

fast • rapid

father • papa

feather • plim

feed • bay manje

feel • santiman

feet • pye

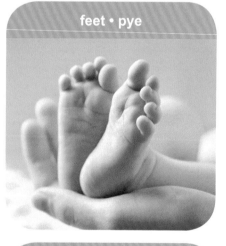

female • fi

fence • kloti

ferry • bato

field • jaden

fig • fig

fight • goumen

file • achiv

fill • ranpli

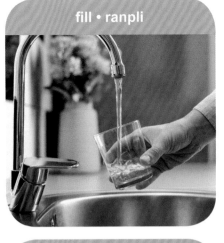

film • fim

find • jwenn

finger • dwèt

fire • dife

**fire engine
kamyon ponpye**

fireworks • fedatifis

first • premye

fish • pwason

fish • peche

A B C D E F G H I J K L M N O P Q R S T U V W X Y Z

A
B
C
D
E
F
G
H
I
J
K
L
M
N
O
P
Q
R
S
T
U
V
W
X
Y
Z

fist • pwen

five • senk

fix • repare

flag • drapo

flame • flanm

flamingo • flamingo

flee • kouri

fling • lanse

flip • lanse

float • flote

flock • twoupo

flood • inondasyon

floor • planche

florist • fleris

flour • farin

flower • flè

flute • flit

fly • mouch

fly • vole

foam • kim

fog • bouya

foil • papye aliminyòm

fold • pliye

follow • suiv

A B C D E F G H I J K L M N O P Q R S T U V W X Y Z

A
B
C
D
E
F
G
H
I
J
K
L
M
N
O
P
Q
R
S
T
U
V
W
X
Y
Z

food • manje

food chain
chèn alimantè

food web
rezo alimantè

foot • pye

football
foutbòl ameriken

forbid • entèdi

force • fòs

forehead • fwon

forest • forè

forget • bliye

fork • fouchèt

fortress • fòtrès
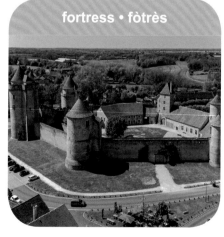

fossil • fosil

found • jwenn

fountain • fontèn

four • kat

fox • rena

fraction • fraksyon

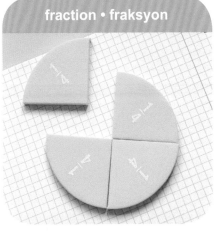

frame • ankadreman

freeze • konjle

friction • friksyon

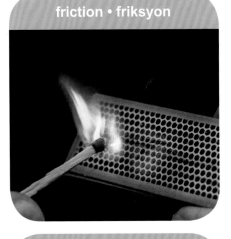

friend • zanmi

frighten • efreye

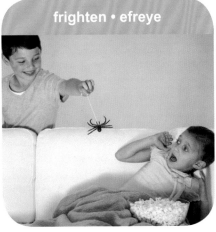

frog • krapo

A B C D E F G H I J K L M N O P Q R S T U V W X Y Z

A B C D E **F G** H I J K L M N O P Q R S T U V W X Y Z

frown • fonse sousi

fruit • fwi

fry • fri

fulcrum • pivo

full • ranpli
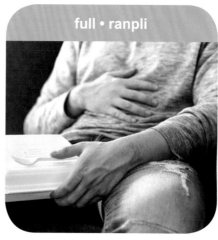

fumes • lafimen

funnel • antonwa

funny • amizan

furniture • mèb

galaxy • galaksi

gallery • atelye penti

gallop • galope

game • jwèt

gap • ouvèti

garage • garaj

garbage • fatra

garden • jaden

garden
pran swen jaden

garland • gilann

garlic • lay

gas • gaz

gasp • sezi

gate • baryè

gather • rasanble

A B C D E F **G** H I J K L M N O P Q R S T U V W X Y Z

A B C D E F **G** H I J K L M N O P Q R S T U V W X Y Z

gaze • rega

gem • pyè presye

generator • jeneratè

germ • jèm

geyser • gayzè

giant • jeyan

gift • kado

giggle • tonbe ri

ginger • jenjanm

giraffe • jiraf

girl • ti fi

give • bay

glacier • glasye

glass • vè

glider • planè

globe • glòb

glove • gan

glue • lakòl

go • ale

goal • gòl

goat • kabrit

gobble • vale

gold • lò

golf • gòlf

A
B
C
D
E
F
G
H
I
J
K
L
M
N
O
P
Q
R
S
T
U
V
W
X
Y
Z

A
B
C
D
E
F
G
H
I
J
K
L
M
N
O
P
Q
R
S
T
U
V
W
X
Y
Z

goodbye • orevwa

goose • zwa

gorilla • goril

grab • kenbe

grain • grenn

gram • gram

grandfather • granpè

grandmother granmè

grapes • rezen

grapefruit • chadèk

graph • grafik

grass • zèb

grasshopper • krikèt

grate • graje

gravel • gravye

gravity • gravite

gray • gri

greater than
pi gran pase

green • vèt

greet • akeyi

grid • kadriyaj

grill • griy

grin • souri

grind • moulen

A B C D E F **G** H I J K L M N O P Q R S T U V W X Y Z

A B C D E F **G** H I J K L M N O P Q R S T U V W X Y Z

grip • pwaye

groceries • episri

groom • lemarye

ground • tè

grow • grandi

growl • gwonde

guard • gad

guard • pwoteje

guess • devine

guide • gide
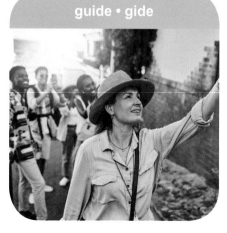

guitar • gita

gulf • gòlf

gun • revolvè

habitat • abita

hair • cheve

hairbrush • bwòs

hairdresser • kwafèz

half • mwatye

hall • sal

halve • mwatye

ham • janbon

hammer • mato

hand • men

handkerchief mouchwa

A B C D E F G H I J K L M N O P Q R S T U V W X Y Z

A B C D E F G **H** I J K L M N O P Q R S T U V W X Y Z

handle • manch

hang • pandye

hanger • sèso

happy • kontan

harbor • pò

hard • di

hare • lapen

harvest • rekòt

hat • chapo

hatch • kale

hawk • lèg

hay • zèb

head • tèt

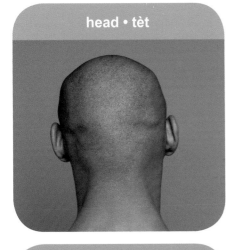

headphone • ekoutè

heap • pil

hear • koute

heart • kè

heat • chalè

heat • chofe

heater • chofrèt

hedge • ranje plant

heel • talon

helicopter • elikoptè

helmet • kas

A B C D E F G **H** I J K L M N O P Q R S T U V W X Y Z

A
B
C
D
E
F
G
H
I
J
K
L
M
N
O
P
Q
R
S
T
U
V
W
X
Y
Z

help • ede

hen • poul

herbivore • èbivò

herd • twoupo

hide • kache

high • wo

highway • otowout

hike • pwomnad

hill • mòn

hippopotamus ipopotam

histogram • istogram

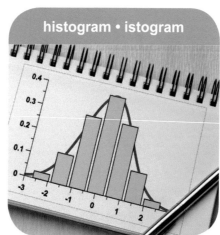

hit • frape

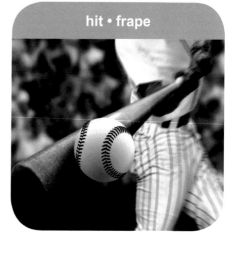

hive • rich abèy

hold • kenbe

hole • twou

honey • myèl

honk • klaksonnen

hood • kapichon

hook • kwochèt

hop • sote

horn • piston

horse • cheval

hospital • lopital

hose • tiyo

A B C D E F G H I J K L M N O P Q R S T U V W X Y Z

A
B
C
D
E
F
G
H
I
J
K
L
M
N
O
P
Q
R
S
T
U
V
W
X
Y
Z

hotdog • òtdòg

hotel • otèl

hour • lè

house • kay

hover • flote

huddle • anbrase

hug • anbrase

human • moun

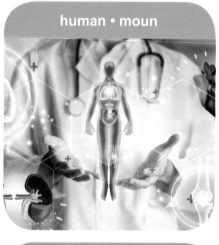

hunter • chasè

hurricane • siklòn

hurry • prese

hurt • blese

husband • mari

ice • glas

ice cream
krèm glase

iceberg • montay glas

idol • idòl

igloo • iglou
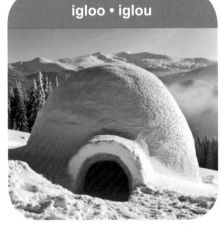

igneous rock
wòch dife

imagine • imajine

improper fraction
fraksyon enpwòp
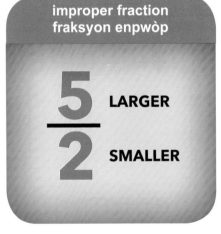

$$\frac{5}{2} \quad \text{LARGER} \quad \text{SMALLER}$$

inch • pous
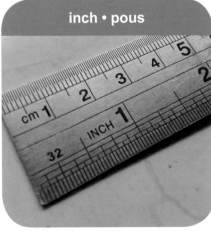

inclined plane
plan enkline

increase • ogmante

A B C D E F G H I J K L M N O P Q R S T U V W X Y Z

A
B
C
D
E
F
G
H
I
J
K
L
M
N
O
P
Q
R
S
T
U
V
W
X
Y
Z

inertia • inèsi

in front of • devan

inherited • eritaj

injection • enjeksyon

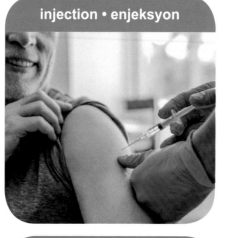

injury • blese

ink • lank

insect • ensèk

insert • mete anndan

inside • anndan

inspect • enspekte

install • enstale

instruct • anseye

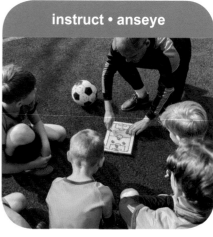

instruments
enstriman

internet • entènèt

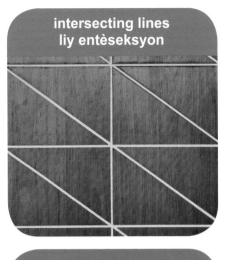

intersecting lines
liy entèseksyon

interview • antrevi

intestine • entesten

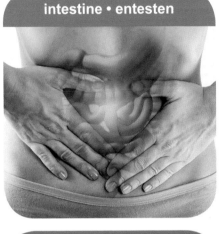

introduce • prezante

invent • envante

investigate
envestige

invitation • envitasyon

iron • fè

iron • fè

island • zile

A B C D E F G H I J K L M N O P Q R S T U V W X Y Z

**isosceles triangle
triyang izosèl**

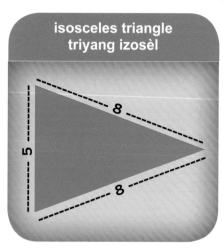

itch • grate

ivory • ivwa

jacket • vès

jam • konfiti

jam • anbouteyaj

jar • bokal

jaw • machwa

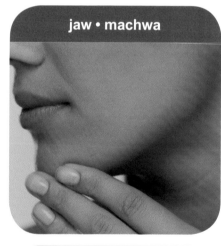

jeans • abako

jelly • jele

jewelry • bijou

jigsaw • kastèt

jog • kouri

join • ansanm

joke • blag

jot • note

journey • vwayaj

jug • galon

juice • ji

jumble • melanje

jump • sote

jungle • jeng

kangaroo kangouwou

kennel • kalòj chyen

A B C D E F G H I **J** **K** L M N O P Q R S T U V W X Y Z

A B C D E F G H I J **K** L M N O P Q R S T U V W X Y Z

ketchup • sòs tomat

key • kle

keyboard • klavye

kick • choute

kilogram • kilogram

kindle • limen

kinetic energy • enèji kinetik
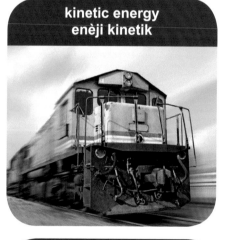

king • wa

kiss • bo

kitchen • kuizin

kite • kap

kitten • ti chat

knead • petri

knee • jenou

kneel • ajenou

knife • kouto

knight • chevalye

knit • trikote

knob • manch pòt

knock • frape

knock down • ranvèse

knot • ne

know • konnen

knuckle • jwenti

A B C D E F G H I J **K** L M N O P Q R S T U V W X Y Z

A
B
C
D
E
F
G
H
I
J
K
L
M
N
O
P
Q
R
S
T
U
V
W
X
Y
Z

label • etikèt

laboratory • laboratwa

lace • lasèt

ladder • nechèl

lady • dam

ladybug • koksinèl

lagoon • lagon

lake • lak

lamb • ti mouton

lamp • limyè

lamp post • poto limye

land • tè

land • ateri

landform • topografi

landslide • avalanch

lane • wout

lantern • lantèn

large / larger / largest
gran / pi gran / pi gran pase tout

larva • lav

laser • lazè

last • dènye

laugh • ri

laundry • lesiv

lava • lav

A B C D E F G H I J K **L** M N O P Q R S T U V W X Y Z

A
B
C
D
E
F
G
H
I
J
K
L
M
N
O
P
Q
R
S
T
U
V
W
X
Y
Z

lawn • gazon

lawyer • avoka

lay • poze

layer • kouch

lead • dirije

leaf • fèy

leak • degoute

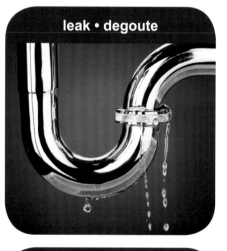

lean • apiye

leap • sote

learn • aprann

leather • kui

leave • kite

left • agoch
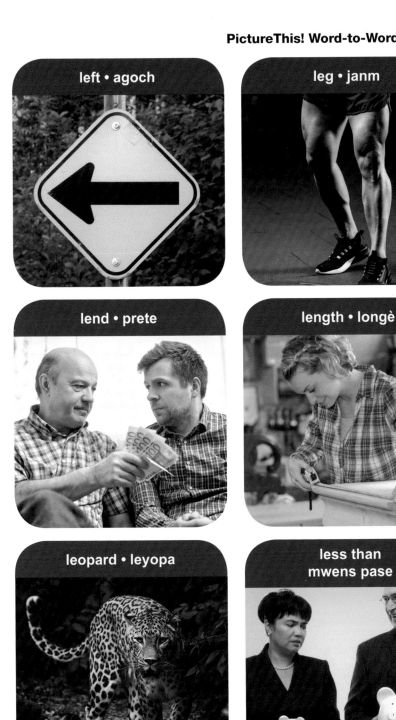

leg • janm

lemon • sitwon

lend • prete

length • longè

lens • lantiy
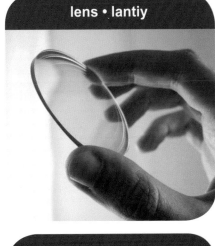

leopard • leyopa

less than mwens pase

let in • lese antre

let go • lage

letter • lèt

lettuce • leti

A B C D E F G H I J K **L** M N O P Q R S T U V W X Y Z

lever • levye

library • bibliyotèk

license • lisans

lid • kouvèti

lie • kouche

life cycle • sik lavi

lift • soulve

light • limyè
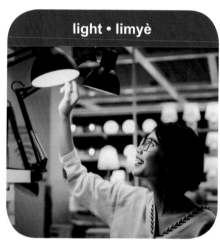

light • limen

lighthouse • fa
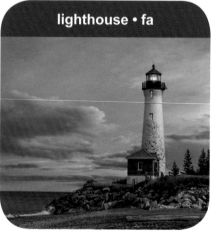

like • apresye

limb • janm
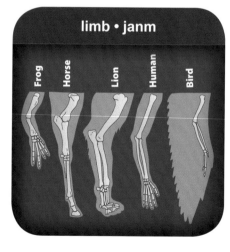

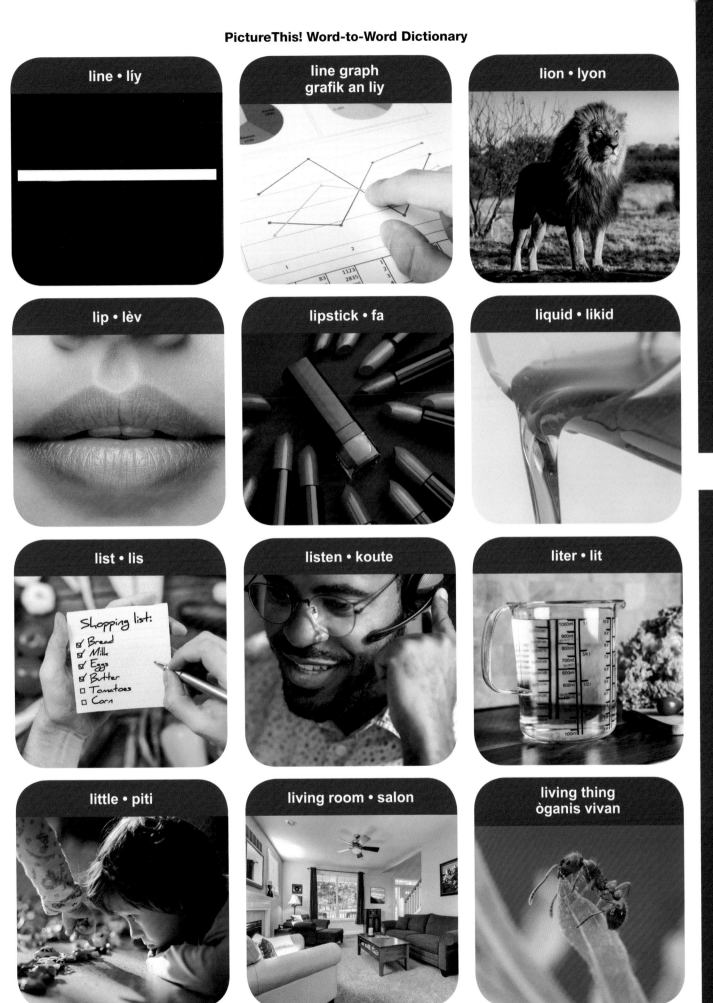

line • líy

line graph
grafik an liy

lion • lyon

lip • lèv

lipstick • fa

liquid • likid

list • lis

listen • koute

liter • lit

little • piti

living room • salon

living thing
òganis vivan

A B C D E F G H I J K **L** M N O P Q R S T U V W X Y Z

A
B
C
D
E
F
G
H
I
J
K
L
M
N
O
P
Q
R
S
T
U
V
W
X
Y
Z

lizard • zandolit

load • chaj

load • mete abò

loaf • pen

lobster • oma

location • pozisyon

lock • seri

lock • fèmen ak kle

log • bwa

long • long

look • gade

loosen • lache

lost • pèdi

loud • fò

love • renmen

luggage • malèt

**lunar eclipse
eklips lalin**

lunch • manje midi

lung • poumon

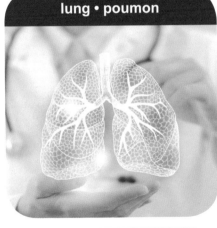

machine • machin

made • fabrik

magazine • revi

magician • majisyen

magma • magma

A
B
C
D
E
F
G
H
I
J
K
L
M
N
O
P
Q
R
S
T
U
V
W
X
Y
Z

magnet • leman

magnetic force
fòs mayetik

mail • kourye

mail • poste

make • fè

mammal • mamífè

man • mesye

mantle • manto

manufacture • fabrike

many • plizyè

map • kat jeyografik

maple • erab

marble • mab

march • mach

mark • make

market • mache

marry • marye

mash • kraze

mask • mas

mass • mas

mast • poto

mat • tapi

match • alimèt

matter • matyè

A B C D E F G H I J K L **M** N O P Q R S T U V W X Y Z

A B C D E F G H I J K L **M** N O P Q R S T U V W X Y Z

mattress • matla

meal • manje

mean • mwayèn
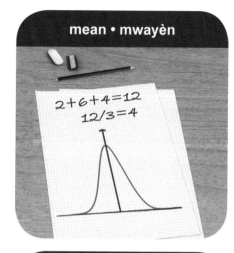

$$2+6+4=12$$
$$12/3=4$$

measurement • mezi

measuring cup
tas pou mezire

meat • vyann

melt • fonn

mend • repare

metal • metal
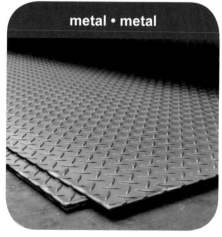

microphone
mikwofòn
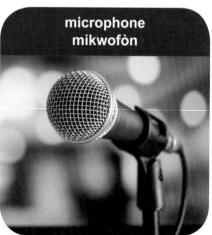

microscope
mikwoskòp
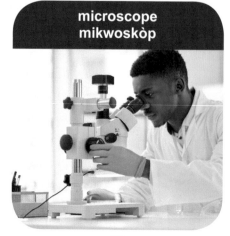

microwave
mikwoond

mile • mil

milk • lèt

mime • mim

mince • tranche

mineral • mineral

mint • mant

minus • mwens

minute • minit

mirror • glas

mix • melanje

**mixed number
nonb miks**

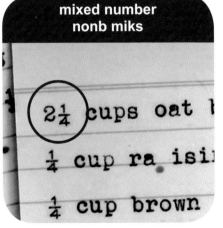

mixture • melanj

A B C D E F G H I J K L **M** N O P Q R S T U V W X Y Z

mobile phone • telefòn mobil

mode • mòd

model • modèl

money • lajan

monkey • senj

month • mwa

monument • moniman

moon • lalin

moon phases • faz lalin

mop • mòp ak bokit

mop • mòp

morning • maten

mosquito • moustik

moth • papiyon denui

mother • manman

motion • mouvman

motorcycle motosiklèt

mount • monte

mountain • montay

mouse • sourit

moustache moustach
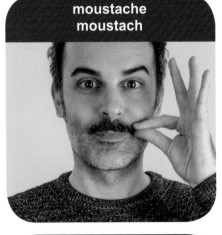

mouth • bouch
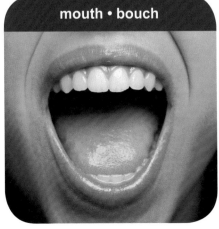

move • bwote

movie • fim

A B C D E F G H I J K L **M** N O P Q R S T U V W X Y Z

A B C D E F G H I J K L **M** **N** O P Q R S T U V W X Y Z

mow • koupe

mud • labou

muffin • ponmkèt

mug • tas

mule • milèt

multiple • miltip

multiplication miltiplikasyon

muscle • misk

museum • mize

mushrooms dyondyon

music • mizik

nail • klou

nail • klouwe

name • non

nap • dòmi

napkin • napkinn

**natural resource
resous natirèl**

nature • lanati

near • pre

neck • kou

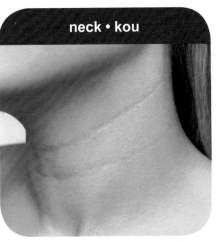

necklace • kolye

necktie • kravat

needle • egui

**negative number
nonb negatif**

A
B
C
D
E
F
G
H
I
J
K
L
M
N
O
P
Q
R
S
T
U
V
W
X
Y
Z

A
B
C
D
E
F
G
H
I
J
K
L
M
N
O
P
Q
R
S
T
U
V
W
X
Y
Z

neighbor • vwazen

nest • nich

net • filè

new • nèf

newspaper • jounal

next • suivan

night • nannuit

nine • nèf

nod • salitasyon

noise • bri

nonliving thing objè ki pa vivan

noodles • espageti

noon • midi

north • nò
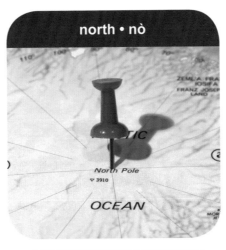

nose • nen
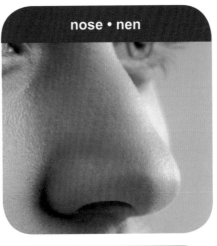

note • nòt

notebook • kaye

nothing • anyen

notice • anons

notice • note

nucleus • nwayo
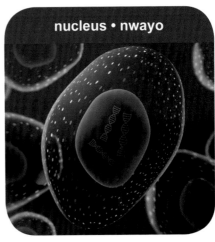

nudge • atire

number • chif

nun • mè
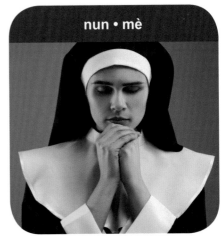

A B C D E F G H I J K L M **N** O P Q R S T U V W X Y Z

nurse • enfimyè

nurse • pran swen

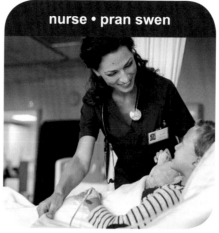

nursery • gadri

nut • nwa

oar • ram

obey • obeyi

**obtuse angle
ang obtis**

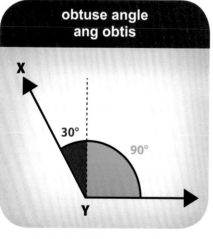

occupy • okipe

ocean • oseyan

octopus • oktopis

**odd number
chif enpè**

off • etenn

A B C D E F G H I J K L M N O P Q R S T U V W X Y Z

offer • ofri

office • biwo

oil • luil

oil • librifye

old • ansyen

olive • oliv

omelette • omlèt

omnivore • omnívò

one • youn

onion • zonyon

open • ouvè

open • ouvri

A B C D E F G H I J K L M N **O** P Q R S T U V W X Y Z

A
B
C
D
E
F
G
H
I
J
K
L
M
N
O
P
Q
R
S
T
U
V
W
X
Y
Z

operate • opere

orange • zoranj

orbit • òbit

orchard • jaden

orchestra • òkès

order • mete annòd

organ • ògàn

organisms • òganis

ostrich • otrich

otter • lout

outcome • rezilta

outside • deyò

oval • oval
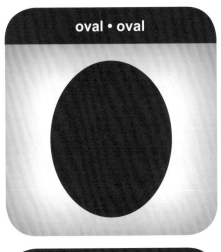

oven • fou

overturn • chavire

owe • dwe

owl • chwèt

own • posede

ox • bèf

pack • anpake

packet • pake

paddle • palèt

page • paj

pail • bokit

A B C D E F G H I J K L M N

O

P

Q R S T U V W X Y Z

A
B
C
D
E
F
G
H
I
J
K
L
M
N
O
P
Q
R
S
T
U
V
W
X
Y
Z

pain • doulè

paint • penti

paint • pentire

pair • pè

palace • palè

palm • pla men

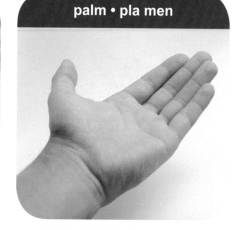

pan • kaswòl

pancake • krèp

panda • panda

pants • pantalon

paper • papye

parachute • parachit

parade • parad

parallel lines
líy paralèl
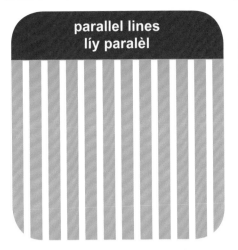

parallelogram
paralelogram
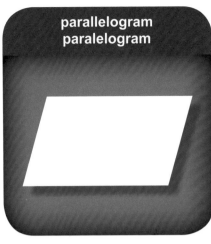

park • pak

park • pake

parrot • jako

part • separe

pass • pase

passenger • pasaje

pasta • pat

paste • kole

pastry • patisri

A B C D E F G H I J K L M N O **P** Q R S T U V W X Y Z

A B C D E F G H I J K L M N O **P** Q R S T U V W X Y Z

patron • kliyan

pattern • patwon

pave • pave

pavement • lari

paw • pat

pay • peye

peach • pèch

peacock • pan

peak • anwo

peanut • pistach

pear • pwa

pearl • pèl

peas • pwa

peck • beke

pedal • pedal

pedal • pedale

peel • kale

peep • siveye

pelican • pelíkan

pen • plim

pencil • kreyon

penguin • pengwen

penny • santim

people • moun

A B C D E F G H I J K L M N O **P** Q R S T U V W X Y Z

A B C D E F G H I J K L M N O **P** Q R S T U V W X Y Z

pepper • piman

percent • pousantaj

perch • poze

perform • jwe

perfume • pafen

perimeter • perímèt
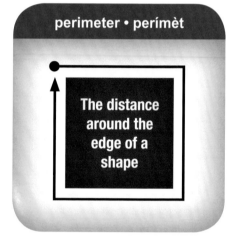

The distance around the edge of a shape

perpendicular lines liy pèpandikilè

pet • bèt kay

pharmacy • famasi

photograph • foto

photograph • fè foto

photosynthesis fotosentèz
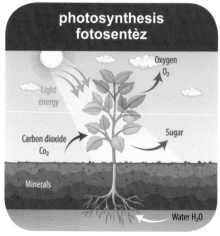

physical change • chanjman fizik

piano • pyano

pick • keyi

pick up • ranmase

picnic • piknik

picture • tablo

pie • tat

pie chart • grafik an sèk

pierce • pèfore

pig • kochon

pigeon • pijon

pile • pil

A B C D E F G H I J K L M N O **P** Q R S T U V W X Y Z

pillar • kolòn

pillow • zorye

pilot • pilòt

pin • zepeng

pinch • pense

pineapple • anana

pink • woz

pipe • pip

pistil • pistil

pitch • lansman

pizza • pitza

place • poze

place value
valè dapre pozisyon

plan • planifye

plane • plan

planet • planèt

plant • plant

plant • plante

plate • plat

platform • platfòm

platypus • platipous

play • jwe

player • jwè

pluck • dekole

A B C D E F G H I J K L M N O **P** Q R S T U V W X Y Z

A
B
C
D
E
F
G
H
I
J
K
L
M
N
O
P
Q
R
S
T
U
V
W
X
Y
Z

plug • ploge

plumber • plonbye

plus • plis

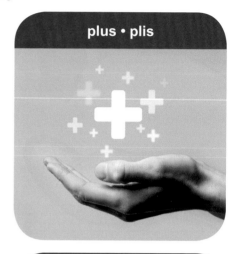

pocket • pòch

poet • powèt

point • pwente

poke • pike

polar bear • lous polè

pole • poto

police • polis

polish • poli

pollen • polenn

pollination polinizasyon

pollution • polisyon

polygon • poligòn
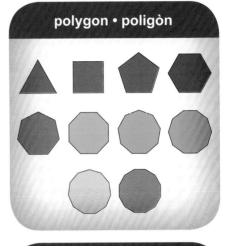

pond • lak

popcorn • pètpèt mayi

population popilasyon
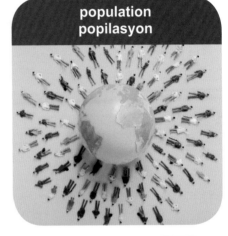

porcupine • do pikan

port • pò
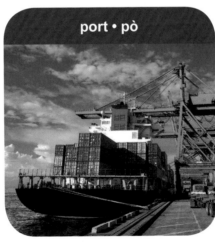

pose • poze

positive numbers nonb pozitif
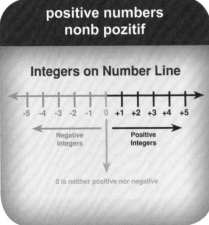

postcards • kat postal

post office • lapòs

A B C D E F G H I J K L M N O **P** Q R S T U V W X Y Z

A
B
C
D
E
F
G
H
I
J
K
L
M
N
O
P
Q
R
S
T
U
V
W
X
Y
Z

pot • bonm

potato • pòmdetè

potential energy enèji potansyèl

pound • liv

pour • vide

powder • poud

powder • poudre
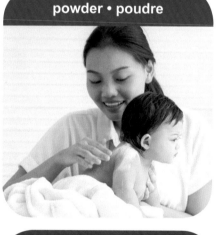

praise • bay lwanj

pray • priye

precipitation presipitasyon

predator • predatè

press • peze

prey • pwa

prime number
nonb premye

prince • prens

princess • prensès

print • enprime

prism • pris

prize • pri

probability
pwobabilite

producer • pwodiktè

product • pwodui

protect • pwoteje

protist • pwotis
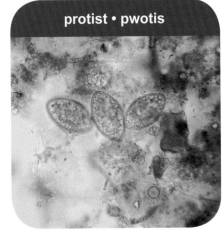

A B C D E F G H I J K L M N O **P** Q R S T U V W X Y Z

A
B
C
D
E
F
G
H
I
J
K
L
M
N
O
P
Q
R
S
T
U
V
W
X
Y
Z

pudding • poudín

puddle • ma dlo

pull • rale

pulley • pouli

pump • ponp

pump • ponpe

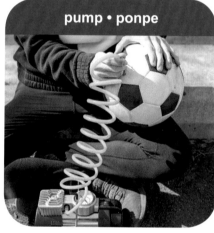

pumpkin • joumou

punch • frape

punish • pini

pupa • krizalid

puppets • maryonèt

puppy • ti chyen

purse • bous

push • pouse

pyramid • piramid

quack • kwen kwen

**quadrilateral
kwadrilatè**

quail • kay

quarrel • fè kont

quarter • yon ka

queen • rèn

quench • satisfè

**question
poze kesyon**

quiet • silans

A B C D E F G H I J K L M N O **P Q** R S T U V W X Y Z

A
B
C
D
E
F
G
H
I
J
K
L
M
N
O
P
Q
R
S
T
U
V
W
X
Y
Z

quit • abandone

quiz • kesyonè
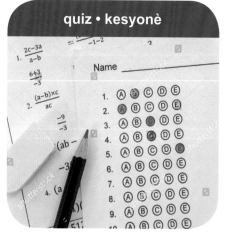

quotient • kosyan
4 sets of 3 apples
quotient of 3

rabbit • lapen

race • konpetisyon

rack • etajè

racket • rakèt

racoon • ratonlavè

radiation • radiyasyon
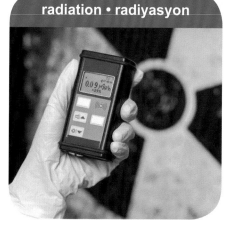

radio • radyo

radius • reyon
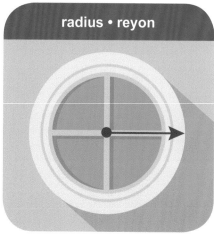

raft • rado

railroad • ray

rain • lapli

rainbow • lakansyèl

raise • leve

raisin • rezen

rake • rasanble

ram • belye

ramp • ranp

raspberry • franbwaz

rat • rat

ray • reyon

razor • razwa

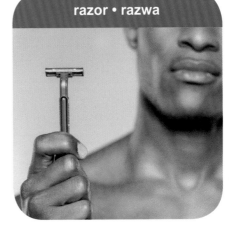

A B C D E F G H I J K L M N O P Q **R** S T U V W X Y Z

reach • rive la

read • li

receipt • resi

receive • resevwa

recline • rekline

record • anrejistre

rectangle • rektang

**rectangular prism
pris rektangilè**

recycle • resikle

red • wouj

**reflect
parèt nan miwa**

reflect • refleksyon

A B C D E F G H I J K L M N O P Q R S T U V W X Y Z

refracts • refraksyon

refrigerator • frijidè

refuse • refize

release • libere

remainder • rès

remember • sonje

repair • repare

**repeating pattern
modèl repetitif**

repel • repouse

report • repòte

reptile • reptil

request • mande

A B C D E F G H I J K L M N O P Q **R** S T U V W X Y Z

A
B
C
D
E
F
G
H
I
J
K
L
M
N
O
P
Q
R
S
T
U
V
W
X
Y
Z

rescue • sovtaj

respect • respekte

rest • repoze

restaurant • restoran
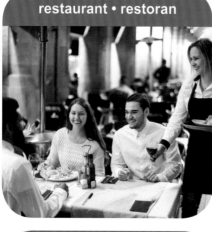

return • retounen

revolution evolisyon

rhinoceros rinosewòs

rhombus • lozanj
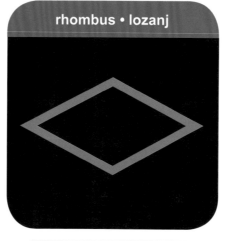

rib • zo kòt
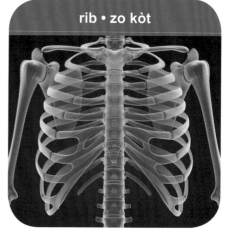

ribbon • tep

rice • diri

ride • monte

right • adwat

right angle • ang dwa

ring • bag

rinse • rense

rip • dechire

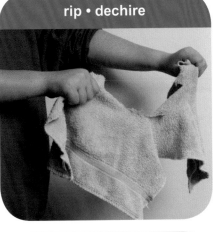

rise • leve

risk • danje

river • rivyè

road • wout

roar • gwonde

roast • griye

robber • vòlè

A B C D E F G H I J K L M N O P Q **R** S T U V W X Y Z

A
B
C
D
E
F
G
H
I
J
K
L
M
N
O
P
Q
R
S
T
U
V
W
X
Y
Z

robe • wòbdechanm

robot • wobo

rock • wòch

rock • dodine

rocket • fize

rolled • woule

roller coaster
montay ris

room • chanm

rooster • kòk

root • rasin

rope • kòd

rose • woz

120

rotation • wotasyon

round • won

row • rame

rub • fwote

ruffle • souke

rug • tapi

ruin • kraze

ruler • règ

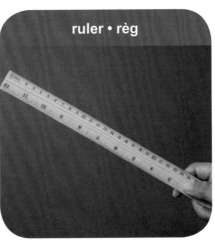

run • kouri

run after • pousuiv

run into • rankontre

rush • prese

A B C D E F G H I J K L M N O P Q **R** S T U V W X Y Z

A B C D E F G H I J K L M N O P Q R **S** T U V W X Y Z

safety • sekirite

sag • koube

sail • vwal

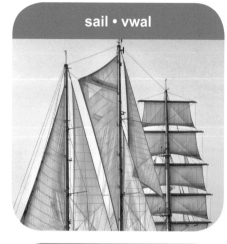

sail • navige

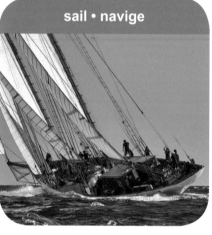

salad • salad

salt • sèl

salute • salye

sand • sab

sandwich • sandwich

satellite • satelit

saucer • soukoup

sausage • sosis

save • ekonomize

saw • si

scale • balans

scare • fè pè

scarf • foula

school • lekòl

scientific methods metòd lasyans

scissors • sizo

scold • reprimande

scoop • boul

scooter • twotinèt

score • rezilta

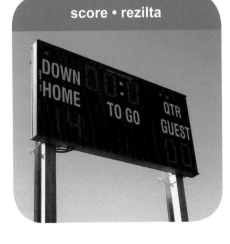

A B C D E F G H I J K L M N O P Q R **S** T U V W X Y Z

A
B
C
D
E
F
G
H
I
J
K
L
M
N
O
P
Q
R
S
T
U
V
W
X
Y
Z

scorpion • eskòpyon

scratch • grate

scratch out • efase

scream • rele

screw • vis

screw • vise

scrub • fwote

sea • lanmè

seal • fòk

seal • fèmen

seasons • sezon

seat • chèz

second • dezyèm

secret • sekrè

sedimentary rock
wòch sedimantè

see • gade

seed • grenn semans

seek • chèche

seesaw • balanswa

select • seleksyone

sell • vann

send • voye

separate • separe

serve • sèvi

A B C D E F G H I J K L M N O P Q R **S** T U V W X Y Z

A
B
C
D
E
F
G
H
I
J
K
L
M
N
O
P
Q
R
S
T
U
V
W
X
Y
Z

server • sèvant

set • ansanm

seven • sèt

shadow • lonbraj

shake • souke

shampoo • chanpou

shape • bay fòm

share • pataje

shark • reken

sharpen • file

shave • raze

sheep • mouton

126

shelf • etajè

shell • kokiy

shelter • refij

shelter • abri

shift • deplase

shine • klere

ship • bato

shirt • chemiz

shiver • tranble

shoe • soulye

shoot • lanse

shop • magazen

A B C D E F G H I J K L M N O P Q R **S** T U V W X Y Z

A B C D E F G H I J K L M N O P Q R **S** T U V W X Y Z

shop • fè acha

shorts • pantalon kout

shoulder • zèpòl

shout • rele

shovel • pèl

shovel • pèlte

show • espektak

show • montre

shower • douch

shower • benyen

shrimp • krevèt

shut • fèmen

shutter • pèsyèn

side • kote

sign • siy

sign • siyen

signal • siyal trafik

signal • fè siy

silver • ajan

similar • menm

sing • chante

sink • lavabo

sink • koule

sip • bwè lantman

A B C D E F G H I J K L M N O P Q R S T U V W X Y Z

A B C D E F G H I J K L M N O P Q R **S** T U V W X Y Z

sister • sè

sit • chita

six • sis

skate • patinaj

skateboard • paten

skeleton • eskelèt

ski • fè eski

skid • patine

skin • po
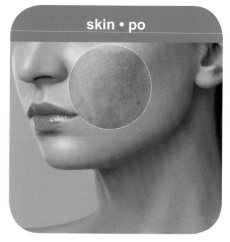

skip • sote

skirt • jip

skull • zo tèt

sky • syèl

skyscraper • gratsyèl

slab • dal

slash • taye

sled • treno

sleep • dòmi

slice • tranche

slide • glise

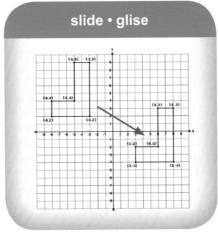

slide • gliswa

slip • glise

slip • bay an kachèt

slippers • pantouf

A B C D E F G H I J K L M N O P Q R **S** T U V W X Y Z

A B C D E F G H I J K L M N O P Q R **S** T U V W X Y Z

slow • lantman

small • piti

smash • kraze

smell • odè

smile • souri

smoke • lafimen

snail • kalmason

snake • koulèv

snatch • rale

sneeze • estène

sniff • odè

snore • wonfle

snorkel • plonje

snow • lanèj

snow • fè lanèj

soak • tranpe

soap • savon

soar • vole monte

sob • kriye

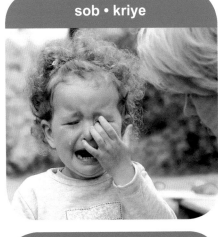

socks • chosèt

sofa • sofa

soft • mou

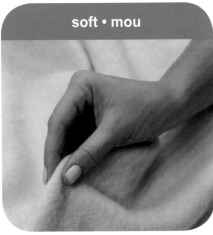

soil • tè

solar eclipse
eklips solè

A
B
C
D
E
F
G
H
I
J
K
L
M
N
O
P
Q
R
S
T
U
V
W
X
Y
Z

A B C D E F G H I J K L M N O P Q R S T U V W X Y Z

solar system • sistèm solè

soldier • solda

solid • solid

solution • solisyon

sort • klase

sort • klase

sound • son

soup • soup

sow • simen

space • lespas

spaghetti • espageti

sparkle • briye

speak • pale

species • espès

sphere • esfè

spider • zarenyen

spill • ranvèse

spinach • zepina

spit • krache

splash • gaye

spoil • gate

sponge • eponj

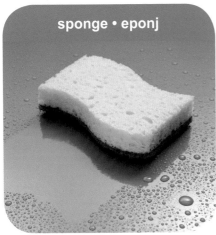

spoon • kiyè

spore • grenn espò

A B C D E F G H I J K L M N O P Q R **S** T U V W X Y Z

spray • flit

spray • flite

spread • pwopaje

spring • prentan

spring • sote

sprinkle • gaye

spy • epye

square • kare

squash • joumou

squat • akoupi

squeeze • prese

squirrel • ekirèy

stack • pil

stadium • estad

stairs • eskalye

stamen • etamin

stamp • poze so

stamp • mete tenm

stand • kanpe

star • etwal

stare • fikse

start • kòmanse

station • estasyon

statue • estati

A B C D E F G H I J K L M N O P Q R **S** T U V W X Y Z

stay • rete

steal • vòlè

steam • bay vapè

stem • tij

step • mache

stethoscope estetoskòp
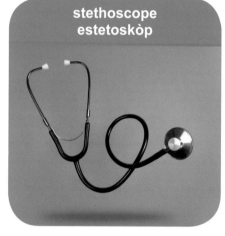

stick • baton

stick • kole

sting • pike

stink • move odè

stir • brase

stitch • koud

stomach • lestomak
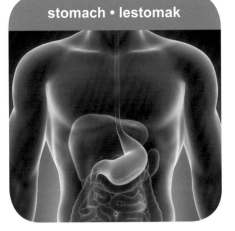

stomp • pile

stone • wòch
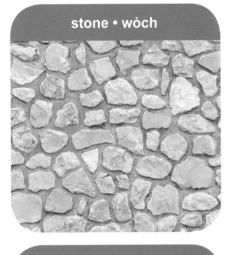

stoop • bese

stop • rete la

store • magazen

store • antrepoze

storm • tanpèt

straight • dwat
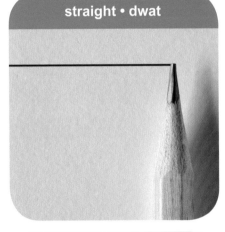

straw • chalimo

strawberry • frèz

street • lari

A B C D E F G H I J K L M N O P Q R **S** T U V W X Y Z

stretch • detire

strike • frape

string • file

stroke • karese

student • elèv

study • etidye

submarine soumaren

subtraction soustraksyon
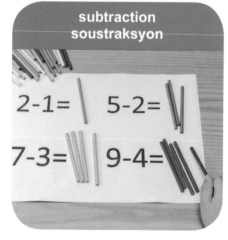

$$2-1= \qquad 5-2=$$
$$7-3= \qquad 9-4=$$

subway • metwo

sugar • sik

sum • sòm

$$75078 + 83408 +$$
$$44190 + 5690 =$$

summer • sezon ete

A B C D E F G H I J K L M N O P Q R **S** T U V W X Y Z

sun • soléy

supermarket sipèmache

support • bay sipò

surprise • sipriz

survey • ankèt

swallow • vale
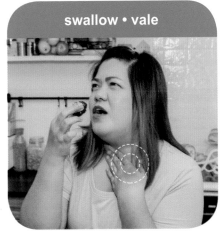

swan • siy

sweat • swe

sweep • bale

sweet • dous

swell • anfle
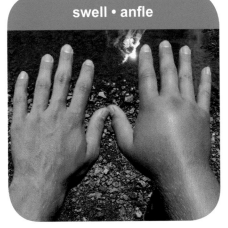

swim • naje

A B C D E F G H I J K L M N O P Q R **S** T U V W X Y Z

swimming pool • pisin

swing • balanse

swing • balanswa

swipe • glise

switch • switch

symmetry • simetrí

syrup • siwo

table • tab

table • grafik

tadpole • teta

take • pran

take off • dekole

talk • pale

tall • wo

tally chart
tablo kontaj

tame • donte

tank • rezèvwa

tap • vire
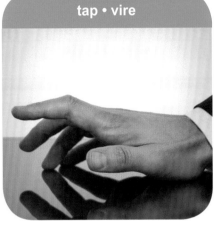

taste • goute

tea • te

teach • anseye

teacher • pwofesè

tear • chire

teeth • dan

A B C D E F G H I J K L M N O P Q R S T U V W X Y Z

A
B
C
D
E
F
G
H
I
J
K
L
M
N
O
P
Q
R
S
T
U
V
W
X
Y
Z

telephone • telefòn

television • televizyon

tell • di

temperature tanperati

ten • dis

tennis • tenis

tent • tant

test • pran tès

thank • di mèsi

thermal • chalè

thermometer tèmomèt

thief • vòlè

think • panse

thread • fil

thread • file

three • twa

three dimensional
fòm twa dimansyon

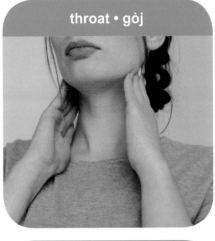

throat • gòj

three • twa image and throat image

through • atravè

throw • lanse

throw away • jete

ticket • biyè

tickle • satouyèt

tidy • mete annòd

A B C D E F G H I J K L M N O P Q R S **T** U V W X Y Z

A B C D E F G H I J K L M N O P Q R S T U V W X Y Z

tie • wozèt

tie • lase

tiger • tig

tighten • sere

time • lè

time • kwonometre

tiny • tou piti

tip • poubwa

tiptoe • pwent pye

tire • kawoutchou

toast • griye

toe • zòtèy

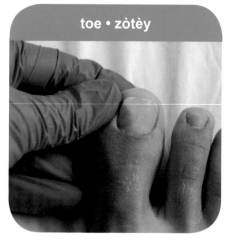

tomato • tomat

tongue • lang

tool • zouti

tooth • dan

toothbrush bwòsadan

toothpaste pat dantifris

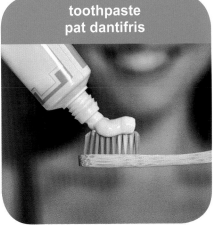

topography topografi

tortoise • tòti

toss • lanse

touch • touche

touch down • ateri

tour • vizite

A B C D E F G H I J K L M N O P Q R S **T** U V W X Y Z

A
B
C
D
E
F
G
H
I
J
K
L
M
N
O
P
Q
R
S
T
U
V
W
X
Y
Z

tow • remòke

towel • sèvyèt

tower • bilding

town • lavil

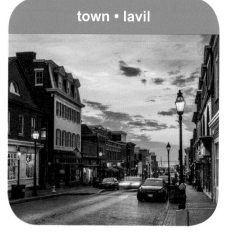

toy • jwèt

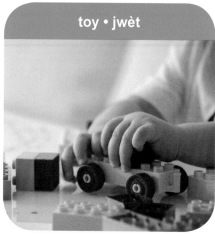

track • pis

tractor • traktè

train • tren

train • antrene

trap • trape

trash can • poubèl

travel • vwayaje

tree • pyebwa

tremble • tranble
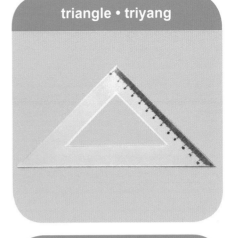

triangle • triyang

trick • riz

trim • taye

trot • twote

truck • kamyon

trunk • kòf

try • eseye

tub • basen

tug • rale

tunnel • tinèl

A B C D E F G H I J K L M N O P Q R S **T** U V W X Y Z

A
B
C
D
E
F
G
H
I
J
K
L
M
N
O
P
Q
R
S
T
U
V
W
X
Y
Z

turn • vire

turn • vire

turn off • etenn
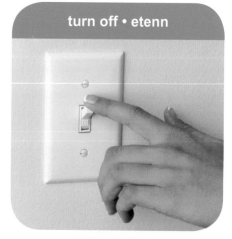

turn on • limen

turtle • tòti

twin • marasa

twinkle • briye

twist • vire

two • de

two dimensional
fòm de dimansyon

type • tape

umbrella • parapli

uncle • nonk

under • anba

understand konprann

uniform • inifòm

universe • inivè
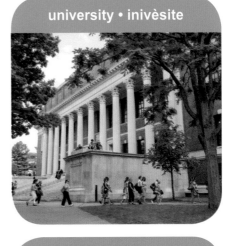

university • inivèsite

unload • dechaje
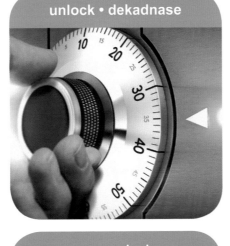

unlock • dekadnase

unpack • debale

untie • demare

unwrap • devlope

up • anwo

A B C D E F G H I J K L M N O P Q R S T U V W X Y Z

upset • fache

use • itilize

utensil • istansil

vaccum
pase aspiratè

vaccum cleaner
aspiratè

valley • vale

value • valè

van • kamyonèt

vase • potaflè
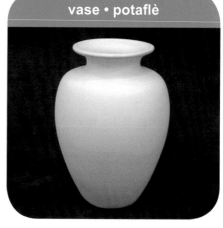

vault • kòfrefò

vegetable • legim

venn diagram
dyagram venn
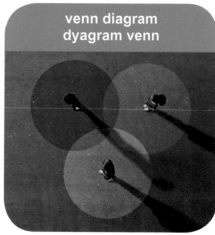

vertex • somè

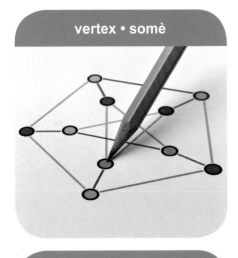

vet • veterinè

vibrate • vibre

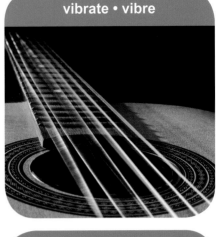

view • gade

village • vilaj

violet • vyolèt

violin • vyolon

visit • vizite

voice • pale

volcano • vòlkan

volleyball • volebòl

volume • volim

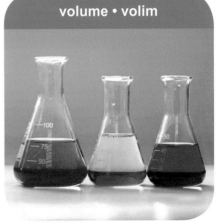

A
B
C
D
E
F
G
H
I
J
K
L
M
N
O
P
Q
R
S
T
U
V
W
X
Y
Z

A
B
C
D
E
F
G
H
I
J
K
L
M
N
O
P
Q
R
S
T
U
V
W
X
Y
Z

volunteer • volontè

vote • vote

vow • jire

vulture • votou

waddle • balanse

wade • patoje

wag • sekwe

wagon • charyo

waist • senti

wait • tann

wake • reveye

walk • mache

walk away • mache alé

wall • mi

wallet • bous

walnut • nwa

wander • flannen

want • vle

warehouse • depo

warm • chofe

warn • avèti

wash • lave

wasp • gèp

waste • dechè

A B C D E F G H I J K L M N O P Q R S T U V **W** X Y Z

A
B
C
D
E
F
G
H
I
J
K
L
M
N
O
P
Q
R
S
T
U
W
X
Y
Z

watch • mont

watch • gade

water • dlo

water cycle • sik dlo

watermelon • melon

wave • vag dlo

wave • fè babay

wear • mete rad

wear out • dechire

weather • klima

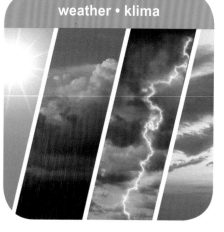

weave • tise

web • twal arenyen

weed • move zèb

week • semèn

weep • kriye

weigh • peze

welcome • akeyi

wet • mouye

wet • mouye

whale • labalèn

wheat • ble

wheel • deplase

wheel • wou

whisper
pale nan zòrèy

A B C D E F G H I J K L M N O P Q R S T U V **W** X Y Z

A
B
C
D
E
F
G
H
I
J
K
L
M
N
O
P
Q
R
S
T
U
V
W
X
Y
Z

whistle • sifle

whistle • souflèt

white • blan

width • lajè

wife • madanm

win • genyen

wind • van

wind • remonte

window • fenèt
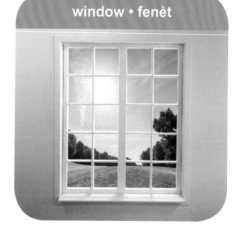

wing • zèl

wink • tiye zye

winter • sezon ivè

wipe • netwaye

wish • swete

wizard • majisyen

wobble • debalanse

wolf • lou

woman • fi

wonder • poze kesyon

woodpecker
zwazo chapantye

wool • lenn

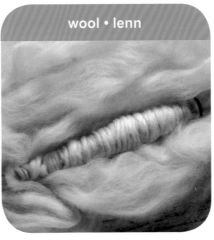

work • travay

workout • fè egzèsis

workshop • atelye

A B C D E F G H I J K L M N O P Q R S T U V **W** X Y Z

A
B
C
D
E
F
G
H
I
J
K
L
M
N
O
P
Q
R
S
T
U
V
W
X
Y

world • lemond

worry • enkyete

wrap • vlope

wrestle • lite

wring • tòde

wrist • pwayè
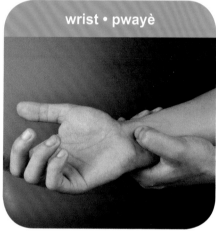

write • ekri

x-axis • aks x
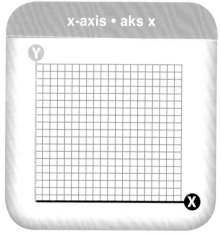

xray • radyografi
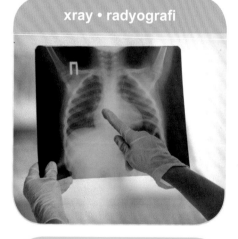

xylophone • zilofòn
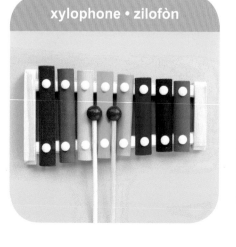

yacht • bato lwazi

yank • sakad